Will This Be On The Final?

Will This Be On The Final?

A poetry volume by Bianca Palmisano
author of "The Empty Spaces"

Cover art by Dave Myles Photography

Copyright © 2016, Bianca Palmisano. All rights reserved. Printed in the United States of America. No part of this book may be used or reproduced in any manner whatsoever without written permission except in the case of brief quotations embodied in critical articles and reviews. For information address aois21 media, LLC, P.O. Box 129, Mount Vernon, VA 22121.

Printed by Lulu.com.

ISBN: 978-1-941771-22-8

Deepest gratitude to Carla Marina Carreira for her keen eye and supportive editing.

To my math teachers, oddly enough.
"There are no weird questions, only weird students."
-Mr. Rylands, Grade 10 Integrated Math

And to my many lovers and friends:
Thank you for all you have taught me.

Table of Contents

1 Freshman

- 3   Out of Practice Love Poem
- 5   Butch
- 7   Paper Heart
- 8   The List
- 10 On Being Told That the Owner of Metropolitan Scooters Will Call Me Back As Soon As He Can
- 12 Phantom Love
- 14 Surprises
- 15 I Want You
- 17 One Act
- 19 Peaches for Eva
- 20 Dateable
- 22 The Toyshop for Broken Girls and Boys
- 24 Spacing
- 25 Semicolon
- 27 4am Swan Song
- 28 Night Train

31 Field Work

- 33 Traveling Aimlessly
- 34 Arrival
- 36 Nairobi
- 38 Nightclub Misgivings
- 40 Kenyan Smooth Jazz
- 42 3rd World Valentine
- 43 Kibera
- 44 Mama, Ukambani
- 45 Re-learning the Country
- 47 Kibera After
- 48 No Saints
- 49 Single Story

Table of Contents

51   **Thesis**

53   Single Story Reprise
55   An Ode To WMATA
57   Every Moment Is Frail
59   Future
60   Little Sister
63   To John Irving, On the Day of My Grandfather's Funeral
65   Afghan Vacation
66   Bro
69   Unsure
70   Meeting You the Second Time

74   **Thank You**
75   **About the Author**

Will this be on the Final?

Freshman

Out of Practice Love Poem

I haven't written a love poem in years
I don't remember how they start

      something about flowers and weather?
      a symphony and butterflies?
      a thousand soaring expectations
      in velvet and chocolate letters...

Arthritic and out of practice,
constantly forgetting my lines
I find beauty in rusted car shells
and burnt out warehouses
the white-washed walls of a kabob house
with old tea on the hotplate.

I forget how to write "Will you Marry Me?"
in jet stream clouds.
My tongue trips over witty compliments
my fluid Italian and French, lost.
Yesterday, I dropped my graceful nonchalance
into soapy dishwater
and marveled at the ripples.

I can't compliment you the way you deserve.
I will compare you to worn-in bedsheets
earthworms, macaroni and cheese
When I meant to say that you glide
with the endless strength of water
wearing away stone,
that your corners are warm
like the blanket that held me through nightmares
and you fill me like bold red wine on a winter night,
all promises and bawdy declarations.
But deep down, you understand me.
You laugh because I remind you
of paprika on chicken nuggets
--spicy, yet familiar--
and when you touch my face it feels
like the contours of an old bruise,
so you hold me gently.

Bianca Palmisano

And you secretly want to take me
into the deepest part of the woods,
nestle me into the ferns and underbrush
where we can sit on a rotting log,
let crickets crawl across our arms,
and tell stories until it is too dark to see.

Butch

Shallow breaths and party hat strings.
We bellow Happy Birthday in discordance.
Your eyes are on me. I don't look away.
Blondes lick cream cheese frosting from their fingers and make wishes
but I arch my body inward to close the space between us.

Humming. somewhere in my chest
as your Bovver boots click,
strident, measured steps in my direction.
I want you to say "kiss me" with your chocolate voice
and hold the soft worm of my tongue between your teeth.
Pulled into needing, my fingers in your shirtstrings,
and I want you to say "stop" like sandpaper,
polishing my edges,
grasp a fistful of my hair and draw me back,
-breathless-

Lit like film noir in the cavern of a crowded room,
we are sliding backwards from candles, beer, stereo clouds
You see me hungry and cock an eyebrow, tell me to touch you.

Sharp inhale.

Fingernails twitching and I enjoin, "where?"

Whose bedroom, which alleyway, and what cliché are we playing
with your leather jacket and silver buckle falling,
your vest and your binder and your dexterous fingers
though we are not quite a cliché
because I am 100% sober
as I unzip you and take your cock,
watching the cinematic contortions of your face
as you grow broader and stronger before me.

You push me against a plaster wall and the world trembles;
outside the party whirls, forgotten because this is what we do—
snatching moments of queerness across party halls and dance floors,
stitching explanations from upturned glances, square-set shoulders
and rapid decisions.

We have no time to waste our living.

You were inside me and now I hold space for you
my spine strung up from your inquest,
my limbs taut and reaching.
I can't move without you,
storing intention in puppet strings and waiting for your lips to decide
what happens next— a kiss, a cell number, the long shadow
of your back facing the hall.

Your softness is unreadable,
as if I could choose from ten thousand adjectives and always
pick the wrong four,
my own voice doubting its echoes.

And suddenly you are all arms, embracing,
your chest solid and tempered, muscles pulsing.
I am condensing, wrapping my coolness around flushed skin,
knitting myself into your contours.
We sift through layers without syllables,
find the doorknob stiff and expectant
turn ourselves in a new direction.

There is no grand entrance, no editorial of sidespent eyes,
only a solitary nod and a coordinated step back into the crowdswell.
We sing happy birthday again,
this time our voices intertwined like one another's gloves.

Paper Heart

On the floor of the classroom
is a paper heart.

At night,
when everyone has gone

I stand in the left ventricle
and spin round and round.

The List

I can't remember
if she said yes or please or ok with a shrug
we met on the train five minutes before passing glances
and rushing back to her flat
falling into the carpet
and not breathing.

And I don't know if she was the same person
when we slid into the men's stall at The Eagle
and she thrust her knee inside my skirt and
grabbed my hair with her fist.

My number is somewhere between 9 and 30
depending on how you count the glances
of that girl across the bar with bright green fingernails
and chewing gum
whose hand will *never* be in my cunt
but whom I might throw against a wall and
bite her neck
making her whisper "fuck me"
in a tiny, shrill voice.

It is in the double digits if you definitively accept
the consultant whose blazer I tore off in the basement
of the Hilton and scratched their back
until it bled small scarlet rivers and they collapsed
into my body with relief.

And it could be nearly 100 if you had seen
all the faces of my wife in the night by moonlight,
whiskey-flooded fingertips and snakeskin inhibitions
a stranger, each time growing warily familiar.

There was the boy from high school
whose name I can't remember
that I'm sure you'd put down for number 2.
I'd rather forget our mismatched expectations
the way my eyeliner smeared when we fucked
and how I coughed, hollow and lonely, the whole drive home.

But you probably wouldn't count the gentleman
that made me curry and kissed me on the cheek
when he left
at 9pm yesterday,
strawberries and champagne still in the fridge
though I taste the twist of his knuckles
covered in garlic long after he's gone.

No matter how you tally
my numbers never seemed to match the stories
told over cocktails and in sleeping bags
long after the grown-ups had gone to bed
and I never understood the rules for counting
who was one and who was five
and who was nothing...
nothing
nothing at all.

On Being Told that the Owner of Metropolitan Scooters Will Call Me Back as Soon as He Can

For once, every reading for my Tuesday 8:45 class is done.

The laundry cleaned, dried, pressed, and folded.

My poem for creative writing class is written
and I have returned the email which has been sitting in my inbox
since last month.

The apartment is vacuumed and I have called my mother.

Everyone has bad days, bad weeks even,
so I feel I should complacently tolerate the coat of exasperation
varnishing my life of late:
my consistent failure
to catch the bus,
to remember my glasses,
to find the remote to the TV
inexplicably lost in my 100 square meter apartment

Yet I cannot get my repressed adolescent impatience past the fact
that it is now ten minutes and thirty-five seconds past one o'clock

and that bastard has still not called.

I have been up and down Wisconsin Avenue half a dozen times,
chasing titles and certificates, locks and goggles,
cutting off drivers of much larger vehicles at the Western Avenue
roundabout in a desperate attempt to find my exit and my sanity,
but I am no closer now to the tags for my scooter than I was
at 11:45 on Sunday morning when I bought the damn thing.

I have anger management class in forty-five minutes,
and if that sad, confused little man calls
    with his dreadlocks
    and spectacles
    and apologetic tootsie roll smile—

Will this be on the Final?

my voice mail will tell him
that he can
fuck himself.

Phantom Love

I surface from my work, floundering,
fear palpable in the nervous fingering of paperclips—
an ache in my chest pushing at the spaces
where she loved me,
daring those muscles to release,
to extend precious inches toward her cheek

I couldn't say "love" to her
bit my lip and held silent in that moment because
I couldn't be sure that I felt it,
knowing only expansive gratitude
my lungs ballooning to take in her deep kisses
and that pinprick of spasm when we let go,
a lingering sense of failure that my own heart
had not grown so magnanimously large

She kissed my eyelids
and held my face as precious glass between her working hands
calluses gently palming my beveled edges
hushing the terror and uncertainty with a finger's firmness
and said goodbye with the unyielding grace
of a child who lovingly released so many kite strings
to the winds of chance

Maybe love is not mine tonight
because it is not weighed like baking flour
nor unrolled like an education
but rather grasped like a cold hammer
and tilted like a paintbrush,
the capacity for art born and labor earned

I have not toiled for love,
nor grown gifted by its grace
so I left her like a child leaves,
shame-faced and resistant,
took the back roads home to a world
which did not stretch my heart in unfamiliar ways

And like children growing wise,
with resonance and solitude
there is doubt.

Maybe this *is* love,
this longing that pursues us in the nighttime
forcing us into new layers of skin
as we bundle up against the darkness
which is too deep and lonely,
the phantom arm that circles us
and squeezes hard,
wakes us with heart-stopping clarity
and chills,
dries our tears when we realize, at last,
how vast and cold the bed is tonight without them

Surprises

There are things in this world that still surprise me:
the girl on the bicycle, crying, as she zooms past
and the man that says "Clarence, hello" at the corner of a stoplight
as if our mothers were old friends
or the tiny drama that plays out in your mind when I say
I love you but I need space right now
as I push you against the bathroom sink and take all of you
from the inside.

Like a kaleidoscope suddenly stilled,
you come into focus piece by piece
and the tension brings me back to myself—
all sadness and whispers and joy.

I want you.

Madly. Voraciously.
Momentarily.
With a wildness that rushes forth without thought from my cunt
gnashing teeth and curling toes and thrusting my breast forward
for you to feast upon in passion.

I want you.
Quietly. Tearfully.
In the vastness of cold bedsheets and endless mountains of blankets
with the TV playing late at night so there are voices when I feel small
your warm body against me

I want you.
Gracefully. Gallantly.
Like cello music playing Chopin and Chambord in tiny crystal
glasses
small footsteps pouring milk at 3am in the edges of my dreamscape
whispering 'help' when the sunset is too beautiful to bear.

I want you.
Unexpectedly. Gently.
As kindness from a stranger at the bus stop after a crushing call
your fingers tracing the inadequacies that pump through my
temples
kissing them away, one at a time.

You are my crash course in taking chances
drinking life in fast gulps of icy water
forcing me into colorful, unfurling recreations of self
always reaching for the next surprise, another fearless leap,
a shuddering sunrise.

I have yet to regret your opportunity,
enticing me with nimble hands to grab hair by its root and pull,
riding bareback and wild across the great western cities.

I want you.
Peacefully, mildly.
In meditation of life's fragile quickness

the way the ladybug remembers last week's picnic of red peppers
and cured sausage
because she might not taste another
your voice nudging me to roll the dice at my turn.

Even when I lose grip, spiraling like spiders torn from their masterpieces,
and sentenced down the cresting waterfall
I tumble into our latest adventure,
another breath of startling mountain air
asking piercing questions of your open spaces,
refusing to plot the coordinates of my next expansive step forward.

I want you.
Passionately. Selflessly.
A thousand miles downstream from your latest demons
singing tenderness into teacups at breakfast time,
embracing the uncertainty of the next morning, and the one after that,
thousands of pancakes to spoon onto your cast iron griddle,
each a different flavor than the last.

One Act

    "It's impossible to stop kissing you"
    and the world ceases to spin when ze says it
    my need converging on their back
    that patient skin holding its breath
like velvet curtains about to part
lips pursed and gaze steady to the balconies,
perpetually ready for grand pronouncement

The opera is about to begin
and the first act is bright blinding spotlights,
clarinets and sousaphones and heady laughter,
    carpet burn and deep kisses
We are the actors, powdering in the wings
the prop master rummaging the basement for feathers,
the crumbling theater cornerstones lettered with wrong dates

    The bay windows are a stage,
    my body pressed against the glass
    and their hands playing trumpet notes 1,2,3
    on my breastbone and projecting me
    into an audience of thunderstorms and urban vistas
I am the grand crescendo,
the A above high C in endless climax,
the expired pages of the score littering the ground

And the stagehands collecting abandoned programs,
sweeping the talcum and dirty footprints,
    me, gathering my clothes from the floor,
    their eyes examining me for traces of sadness

Because there only *is* one act
but sometimes I forget and mix in pages
from old scores, sketches that didn't fit the draft
I tack on an aria, withhold a verse
and call, even after I promised I would not

There is only one act and yet somehow
I forget the blocking every time:
that ze stands here and I stand there
and we do not need to scrape hips

as we pass downstage left where
my heart is balanced precariously atop stilts

There is only one act but for some reason
it was different when you picked up and started singing
where we did not belong

And we did not answer to the conductor,
waving frantically at his script
or the audience thumbing their translations, confused,
but made our own music to follow,
added glissandos and swift, dramatic trills
rewrote the inevitable estrangement,
and left the heartbreaking finale to the next cast.

Peaches for Eva

For Christmas, I bought you two unexamined peaches.
I do not know if their skin was slick or their muscle full of brown patches.
You didn't check.

I gave you two peaches and you
dug out the pits and traced each of their ridges with your tongue.

You let their edges scratch you, peel back your cheek with broken blood vessels
sucked deep on the painful divots
and gave me back the sweet flesh to taste.

Dateable

I can see why people might date me.
I am sparkling, riotous, jubilant.
My kisses are animal and coffee-tinted.
I dance in supermarket aisles.
I wear bespangled hats and make faces in photo booths.
I am eminently dateable.

I can see why people might keep me around.
I garden love and soft touches; I remember birthdays.
I stroke your hair and say "hush baby."
I bring you dark chocolate and play Mozart on scratchy records
and remind you why you're too good
for that job
        that man
                that byline in bold typeface.
I will let you be fragile, if you whisper urgently that you need me.

I can see why people need me.
We are broken, fragile, lonely, forgotten.
We are every empty barstool and unreturned love letter.
We are big, bold, blaring mistakes when everything was on the line.

But you.
You never needed.
You were all-stitched-together in a three piece suit, whiskey sour,
and a promotion.
You were cooking your own dinners and making the rent.
You were published. Known.

I ... couldn't see why you'd keep me around.
You didn't need ice cream or hush baby or off-key, drunken serenades
or 1am angry sex because fuck him and his fiancé in Idaho.
You just wanted me.

And I have a hard time accepting that as a fair bargain.

Because you grill chicken and peel bandaids and buy suit coats
and still hold me when I am dying inside.
You scrub shower mold and mend promises
and kiss me on the forehead and say "beautiful"
and somehow

I have to believe that I'm enough.

The Toyshop for Broken Girls and Boys

Like children in the world's oldest toy shop,
we found each other amidst the doll heads and spinning tops,
wrapped arms around one another's mysteries,
became bold when they told us to be gentle,
gentle when they told us to be cold.

You with the tinkerer's hands,
who could bring stuffed bears to dance and old blocks to sparkle
wove with your words and painted with your smile,
wrote me love in the tinkle of toy bells
that sang through every corner of our small world.

It was you who dusted off the shelves of heartache
like a game of hide-and-seek,
pulling your sleeve through the cobwebs
to see what fragile emotion was boxed there.
It was you who sifted the mismatched gears,
the wiry, rusted-out intention,
and built a music box to harmonize our voices.

You didn't notice when the notes cracked,
the hinges of my heart needing salve and kisses,
only entreated me to lift my voice and chorus with you,
showering tenderness upon all the misfit toys.

You found each iteration of my self
and held it like glass marbles,
blessing the spectral colors and kissing the reflected light,
polishing each imperfection and packing it away
for the perfect moment of play.

Your touch feels safe and destined,
like the treasure map I have been studying since birth,
and I know your movements like the creases of the closet
where I used to hide myself,
praying always for more time between rounds.

You understand me as if we were on purpose,
yet we are not a well-chosen hand of cards or a skillful game of chess,

our sculpted shadows stepping calculated across checkered pasts,
nor a puzzle with defined, requisite edges,
but some ethereal wind sounding like chimes,
your heart racing mine to the beat of a new adventure.

If moments can be anniversaries,
then we have lives 20 lifetimes in the creation of this closeness,
crafting new memories of wood and string,
scraps of daydream pressed fresh against the gritty walls of old expectation.

This love doesn't feel like sleeping,
a collective fantasy bundled snug against life's drawn exterior,
but if it were a dream and I woke,
I would try to find you,
searching faces in subway cars and grocery lines
for eyes that know my contours like a time-worn wooden flute,
those nimble fingers that hold my heart on tiny puppet strings.

and a sunset that burns it all off
and that great indifference
between me and you
and the pinprick and the cherry blossom
The space between me
The space between you and god
The space between you and I
I believe in the spacing

thoughts in unusual ways
the mind tracing
the erratic
in the spacing
important
but there was something
it felt like a gimmick
and
from the end backwards
I wrote this poem

Spacing

Semicolon

I need you to be here today,
to see me smile at strangers on the train
and tip 25% at the counter-service deli
to notice how I winked at the canvasser on 14th St
and planted seeds of friendship in unsolicited Facebook messages.

But I need you to see that I am not always my rainbows.
That I am not always my politics
And sometimes I fucking hate people for no reason at all
and I'm not sure that I'm sorry

I need to articulate that I will probably fail you spectacularly
-Again-
that my expectations draw blazing lines into the horizons
and sometimes they burn at your touch.

I am no better at this than I was 5 years ago.

It is unfortunate that my worst days are not my sad ones,
my grief rolling over itself in waves,
but mornings like this,
where I can only recite the catechism of my own selfishness,
all the verses where my needs subsume yours.

Some days I am definitely not a good enough person for you,
but I need you to see the way my stomach spasms
when I have to give bad news,
even when it's my own judgment pouring out in buckets of
inarticulate criticism

And I need you to see that I spend those afternoons thinking of how
you'll describe me when you leave,
the poems you'll write or the summary you'll give to consoling
friends
--she was sweet and tender, but she wanted too much, her edges
were too sharp--
because the way I bruise you,
I can't figure you'll stand by for another round.

But maybe that's exactly how we're the same,

writing the tragic conclusion of a story we're only half way through,
fighting for something tidy in a middle that's painful,
because a period is always easier to draw than a semicolon between thoughts.

I don't think we're done here,
but I guess we have to believe
that our dysfunction is worth fighting for,
that even if we are broken and pointy
there is time to file down the corners and glue the seams.

I need you to see the way my poor heart screams
     don't go, please dear god don't go
every time you smile at me,
the hands that hold you tighter when it hurts
because they know there is something steady even in our failings,
the teeth that have torn at the gullet of trauma before and stood up
bloodstained but victorious,
and all the fight I still have in me to make this work.

There is no love stronger than the one that says Yes when it easier to walk away cold.
It's freezing, but I'm still here.

4am Swan Song

It is 4am and I am staring at my lifelines
waiting for them to cross with yours,
retracing my lips on your book bindings
and inhaling your dance steps, pressing 1,2,3 deep into me.

It is 4am and I am weaving the pieces of my comforter undone
instead of hurting
holding out for penance from the blackbird
that flaps its wings within my eyelids
when I am yearning for sleep to erase your visage.

It is 4:30am and I am reaching the infinite divide
between you and the restless tile
feeling instinctively for your grooves
those dark snakes that encompass my passing
as I travel the long hallways of insomnia.

It is 4:45am and I am pressing my face against the window pane
to feel my skin recoil and stiffen
my fibers tightening around you in stillness
as I gather myself in the face of the moon

It is 5am and I am learning not to fight the way my insides soften to embrace you
my lungs concave and my stomach soft
to accept your punishment,
quiet yet resilient,
taking no rests.

It is 5am and melancholy brings forth your face
so I will encircle it gracefully
bending like a swan to cover the ache between my ribs,
hold it a little more tightly.

Night Train

Some days I miss you like rain
with a chill that raises my skin and draws me into myself,
elbows and chest to prickling knees
and I find my kitchen too staid without your singing,
your skirts twirling to a hymn only you can hear.

Some days I miss you like candlelight
when the power surges and the night falls away,
electric hum exposing oily corners and flaking paint
and I remember how vast and splintered my life remains.

Some days I miss you so much that I pack a toothbrush
and catch the night train at 12:15am and find myself
pacing the long, wide range of your farm town,
waiting for the bus to pass with its chrome siding,
its seats smelling of mudwater and hay.

Raise your hand if this was not part of the plan:
this midnight ascension,
arrival to an ascetic room with bare ceiling and creaking chairs,
the communal confession at this spare wooden table,
staring blankly at the asparagus,
wondering how I got here at 5am with a ring in my hand,
mortgaged off the carcass of my old Pontiac Cruiser.

Raise your hand if you were accustomed to my meticulous planning,
starched ledger books and precise budget lines,
measured guideposts on the long run to the life I'm meant to be living.

Don't remind me that I don't have the $7 and 53 cents for a return
to that cold flat in Brighton with the strange satin curtains and stale, iced deli meats
or that the landlord must wonder why I never pick up my mail on Saturdays.

Don't remind me that "yes" doesn't erase 200 miles of countryside
or a dilapidated economy of sentiment,
spread thin over months of empty paychecks and twice-rung teabags,

that "I love you" is not the same as future,
no matter how round her voice rings across the hillsides when she says it.

Give pause instead to the great white hope of this threadbare room,
knowing that grandparents and children have done it before us
run off with their pennies into a fairytale,
never looking back at the world they tilted on its side.

Hope, even, for a god with kind puppet strings,
wild and fanciful,
that lifts our hands from the obvious choices,
and brings down the curtain before we can fall.

Will this be on the Final?

Field Work

Travelling Aimlessly

There seems to be no help for
the length of my poems,
I think,
as I ride a German train
southbound towards a city
with some inscrutable foreign name

Arrival

I am brazen like the new day,
sharing the consequences of a 12-hour plane ride
and my first case of food poisoning (so far)
with the only other wazungu in Kenya.

We like to pretend that we already know where we are,
marveling at the boy on the bicycle,
too ingenious to peddle,
dangling from the bumper of a semi on A108,
as our tire flatlines. Eleven startled white faces
wish there was an Eagle Scout among them.

We are scared of the black men
that follow us, eyes full of dangerous curiosity,
as we wander a Brave New World
full of glass shards and unleaded fuel,
but in a month's time we will just be pissed off,
because the same men still have eyes
of dangerous curiosity, having absorbed none of what we are
while we've breathed in all of them.

But right now, we are finding
that Nairobi has houses the color of Easter eggs
and there is grass to be smoked in this crumbling city,
but that doesn't mean we should bother,
and the Masai love booming sound systems
almost as much as their church music
and most of all,
the deafening explosion of faith
from the two combined.

We are learning to always jump back from mud puddles
because drivers do not care if you are wearing a new shirt,
nor do they care about stop signs,
or seatbelts or turn signals,
and we will have to adapt.

We are learning never to pay more
than 70 shillings to get to Westlands,
especially if the driver gives us that funny look,

and to remember how Naivasha smelled
when we got off the bus on day 1,
like monsters and hydrangeas and adventure,
just waiting for us to arrive.

Nairobi

Nairobi breathes gridlock
a hedgemaze of exotic, diesel-stained streets
where I recognize nothing but the constancy of stares
and the rumble of alien conversation.

It is not for me.

It could have been any city
or no city at all
except every face was black,
all the landmarks gone,
leaving me floundering in the exhaust,
coughing up haze and disillusion.

There is no anger, only frustrated resistance
to the pedestrian struggle of midday
Everything is ordinary—
but I am not expected to belong.

Wandering confronts me with Kenyatta,
then Moi,
bylanes of dead presidents shouting Harambe!
into the corners of this dark continent,
the streets filling with Technicolor
Bangles, Chicken, Lipstick, Fries,
endless green and white Safaricom
emblazoned on every corner.

This place is not mine.

And though I know intimately
that there is no Starbucks, no TJ Maxx
with overflowing aisles of discounts,
I still look for home in the dust,
in the faces of strangers I will never meet.

Keep walking,
and with each step, a heartbeat,
a sharp gasp of nerves and inspiration,
reminding the body to expand,

to take in the anonymous strangeness,
to become corporeal, despite disorientation
to inhale problems and exhale solutions.

I don't know where I'm going
and that is okay.

Nightclub Misgivings

Lit starkly,
she is porcelain in a pool of ebony,
languishing in the sweat and heat and dust
that consumes you
she lingers—pristine, immaculate
untouchable white lace in a marketplace full of black nylon.

Roaring down Uhuru Highway,
petulant and impatient,
her closet full of four inch heals unfit
for any road in Nairobi,
you become one black face in a million
watching her evaporate
into clothing stalls and Chandaria books.

You barely breathe
for her beauty and the fumes
that belch from matatus during rush hour
and perpetuate day-dreams of dancing,
long, liquid hours of nighttime with her
pumping rhythm into your hips
arresting your heart with every half-beat.

Your lips are close,
blowing Tusker and cigarettes,
and suddenly she pulls you away
from the rush and beat and lights,
into an alley, out of sight from the cabbies
waiting to rip off young girls with porcelain skin
who should never be in alleyways with
men like you.

She is all hands, wild like hair
let loose in the Masai Mara,
and you are only consent,
"yes" whispered bodily into the throbbing night,
swirling spit and spirit in endless rotations
You become pure and white as fresh-driven snow
and she black as the foreboding night sky.

When it is over, you both wonder which has
perpetuated the fiction they wanted to erase
the beast in the girl who wants a black man for his sex
or the beast in the man, who wants the girl for her color.

Kenyan Smooth Jazz

The club plays Kenyan smooth jazz,
and pours endless Tusker
cold because you're
    mzungu mjinga
200 bob extra because no one will
tell a white girl the real price

Kwani busts rhymes and you
almost forget that you can't walk home
streets littered with
    thieves and bandits
    and you wouldn't know
what else might be hiding

Even daylight has its price now—
purses slashed, cameras filched
by nimble fingers
even though you think you know
exactly where you're walking
    what matatu you need
    what corner of River not to wait at

You're a cream-flavored target,
plus 2000 ksh and a Blackberry
And this is Nairobbery,
didn't they tell you
in your guidebook?

Not a tourist? Says you.
This is Pangani, not Westlands,
not Karen, not your homininy-colored
suburb of expats and misfits

No one cares how dirty
you sling your sheng,
    how long you've slummed in Koch,
    how many nights this week you ate sukuma
and ugali that you cooked by hand

Will this be on the Final?

Your skin is milky
and your foreign breath smells arrogant

So stick to shopping at Yaya
and trips to the Bomas
your plane will be here soon
and you can leave these savages
                        BEHIND.

3rd World Valentine

It costs 3 shillings to say I love you
at the rate we talk,
our voices crawling across the Atlantic
on old, static handsets.

    The hands I'd hold you with are dusty
    and my tongue is sandpaper,
    turned rough with lack of use.

This place carved suspicion into love,
me, guarding your visage with grease-covered claws,
but forgetting what it means to trust you
    you, hesitating before my questions
    balking when my grief held you too tight

I took this post with naïve fantasy,
packed my belongings in a ratty duffle
and kissed you goodbye too quickly,
anticipating adventure, redemption
    a trans-continental romance
    the beginning of our opus.

These days I'm afraid to call,
to crack open my flaws and crusting heart
detail the collapse of my sacred ambition
    your soul wanted divinity
    and I could not deliver you

I am not youth or joy or compassion
riding her white horse, vestments flowing
here to ferry love to the decaying world
    and you are not reason, (mammoth as I supposed)
    strong chin full of pointed determination

We are just people,
crying on opposite ends of the world
gnashing at dreams that were never real
loving each other because we're supposed to.

Kibera

Enter Kibera.
And a million reasons to have stayed home.

Apathy slides off like the sweat of a drowsy man,
lying in the dust and the heat like wood scrap
(I thought he was **dead**)

I refuse to acknowledge either side
of Kibera's insular dual city
not the mama with fresh mangos spoiling in the sun
nor the matatu conductor with his glove compartment full of cash

I walk around, reciting sick notes in Swahili
dredging for direction among the second-hand clothes at Toi,
trying to break off a piece of Africa for back home
waiting for enlightenment—heat stroke—
to blind me with icy-white clarity.

I am only one set of eyes
seeing two sets of tragedies:
the way the West failed to save "them"
and how they keep getting up again
without the sense to see they are dying.

Are they dying?

I am lost.
And if Kibera is found, then so be it
lost I remain.

Part of me can't face their ugliness.
All of me can't face mine.

Mama, Ukambani

Sing to me and I can feel you
stirring until I am smooth porridge
sliding into you, feeling your quiet,
yielding strength.

Sisemi Kiswahili kwa sababu najifunza
It is always better to watch than to speak.

I know nothing, offer nothing,
yet you stuff me with kuku,
embe, mbuzi, chai
all the sweetness of home
spread wider – a soul's harvest
swaddled in human softness
warm blankets on a wooden bedstand
a dull ache that I couldn't be more.

I have a million poems, waiting,
unfinished in books like this
yet I return to yours
chasing chickens out the door
filling buckets at the borehole
eating sweet potatoes and blue band
while daylight fades like a storybook ending
dusky, slanting glow and all.

I am in love with the sunset,
the velvet night, the vacuous sky
the hills that refuse words
and force me to stare
long and hard into the distance
awaiting future's clarity and reprieve.

Re-learning the Country

I haven't smelled frangipani
since the Brussels perfume shop.
I haven't seen a lion
bound across the Serengeti
nor listened to the hum
of cicadas in the baobab trees.

If I rescued the natives from their squalor, they didn't recognize it.

I learned Kenya from the wrong textbook,
and now it is re-teaching me

with cold showers after a dusty commute
fragmented lectures echoing on sterile linoleum
burning trash clouds billowing into mid-morning haze
and endless, finger-tapping time.

But I am **resistant**.
Brash. Loud. *Mzungu*. **WHITE**.

Kiswahili trips off my tongue and dirt crusts my feet in rings,
reminding me that I am strange.
I grow dark, but never dark enough.
I do not blend.

Molding myself into Kenya
is slow, heartrending
She creates windows and walls,
and I become impatient wind,
tapping endlessly,
learning to accept the curves of glass
which separate me from a feeling of home.

Currents shift, and I flow Westward,
but a story in me remains:
my skin remembers the startling punch of rain
the summer sap of mango
and the firm grip of a black hand
always pointing, always teaching,

which refused to let me go.

Kibera After

There's unmistakable novelty
in Swahili reggae, fresh tomatoes
and the quintessential Kibera moment
-Olympic, 4 PM, fresh chapati-
that pokes me in the shoulder,
whispering surreptitiously,
"You're mzungu in Kenya
and you're enjoying it too much."

I dipped my foot in sewage this morning
but it doesn't smell too much.

What do you mean, "did I wash it?"

3 months later and a million burdens lighter
Kibera and I have a truce:
I will permit shit on the floorboards
if she will give me twelve hours warning
to pack my gumboots and pull back my hair
for the rainy season.

She hasn't kept her end of the bargain.

If I am productive, it is by accident
and feigned professionalism,
the inspirational combination
of power, internet, and ndengu
from Abondos, washed down with
chlorinated mango juice
and the perplexity of co-workers
unfamiliar with google docs
and dropbox

but happy to ask if America
has blackouts like this one.

"Let's go get tea," I say
these answers aren't simple.

No Saints

The butterflies mourn my loss of optimism,
but no one else does.

I will not return to Kenya and it is for the best.

Sunshine finds strength in the loss,
rejects my want and glows brighter,
refusing pain as it evolves from disillusion
my own quaint search for purpose
on a new continent cut irreparably
from its moorings.

I am not needed here.

There are no saints in Nairobi,
fewer still in the bara or the coast
sniffing the ground for their own redemption
exhausted commodity in a country
less than thankful for our self-aggrandizing charity

Each of us was accosted by the brightness,
bleached ledgers of CDC grants,
opportunity in verdant green vegetable gardens,
dusty charcoal classrooms of equity and self-sufficiency
-false promises and sunburn all-

Reality has bitten loose the heartstrings:
my chest aching for lost dreams, lost direction,
so much less beautiful than my romantic unknowing
wishing back ignorance to engender wonder, false destiny
the dance of hope that stirs a lover onward
to toil, bitterly, without reprieve,
and birth an infinitesimally better life.

This is not my struggle.

It is right that these visions
burn bright and die hard.

Single Story

Mokoko, fried ground nuts, 10 AM
you reach the last five naira note in the coffee can
after 20 months without work,
and munch, pensive,
with the smell of shit on your tongue.

Feel heat like a swollen brother,
sick with kwashiorkor, lying on your back.
Slip on sandals and keep looking,
looking like always, waiting for answers.

Dibia man sits like a prophet in his room
spinning stories about wealth and revenge
handing out recipes in coke bottles ,
washed in the river you spat in.

There's danger in this single story
but sometimes even you forget that
Naija's more than puss and empty bellies,
babies crying, tragedy in their eyes.

Forget The Master, your old VCDs,
forget Saro Wiwa, forget highlife,
forget Kano and Hausa men
with their dirty knives at the throat
of pretty girls and Igbo wives

Forget all the things that could have made you proud.
Lash out in the blankness at an empty future,
the whiteness on the skin of gawkers
and sad, worried faces,
the way they say, "Look how he doesn't even swat
the flies at his eyes."

Lose yourself in your own complicit sorrow,
your substitution of an uncomplicated villain,
and miss the chin chin and suya burning sweetly
in the traffic jam down the canal,
headed somewhere.

Miss the area boys beating the ground with their fists,
the mama in her hijab nursing a new life,
the stomp of bare feet refusing to settle:
a nation collectively holding its breath
for something more than your pity.

Will this be on the Final?

Thesis

Single Story (Reprise)

America with the golden arches,
the vistas, the plains,
the blinding glitter of Vegas

America with Mercedes Benz,
the fine china and too much food
the chicken with no gristle,
with breasts the size of your fist,
tight and juicy and meaty.

America with new suits and air conditioners,
the fine wine and proper ladies,
the big men and crisp English
"Nice to meet you."

maybe,
or

America with the cold stares,
the hoodies and the guns,
the questions about the motherland
and your language and your tribal music
and your dark, mysterious skin.

No one told you about America with the rape,
the incessant rattle of homeless men
breathing out the change they shake
in McDonalds cups on the corner
of 31st and Vine,
where you assumed it would be a peaceful place to think.

No one told you about America with the DMV,
the endless reams of paper slicing your fingers
and white lights blaring, asking for your ID number
and your registration number and your phone number
and the frumpy woman at the counter with the loose breasts
frowning at your dark, mysterious skin.

No one told you about America with the loneliness,
the quiet nights in your one-room apartment
with your gas stove and your macaroni
and your dark, mysterious skin.

Will this be on the Final?

An ode to wmata

Most days, I can't remember what it feels like to be well
my fibers knitted to an everyday exhaustion,
eyelids heavy
breathing low and humid,
the way we wake and count all the Mondays remaining in eternity
before rising.

Yours is the same strain of muscles refusing to engage,
skin pulled taut through too many icy winters,
tracks warped to snapping under the weight of impatients:
always an exasperated sigh, a rolled eye and settled complacency
that yes, yes you *would* make them late again today of all days.

The commute takes a lot out of you.
Hundreds of thousands of bodies pressed tight into high-speed
metallic shrapnel,
your edges sharp and rusty from running the same 108 miles of
track every day.
Being the nation's transit system has always been a dead-end job,
and no mentor has invested in you for 20 years.
So it's no wonder that you pause a few moments extra before
disengaging the breaks on the first run of the morning;
no surprise that you listen for midnight to trigger
the shift whistle each weekday.

And while they'll complain that metro
will make you late to your own funeral,
they don't talk about your own slow descent into sickness,
the way your bones ache with each sunrise,
your blood like molasses, rolling down miles of suburban byway
during morning rush hour--
because they don't remember your Christopher Columbus
discoveries of the 80's,
the triumphant outgrowth of rail you laid down,
planting your flag in neighborhoods no one had heard of until you
resettled them.

But I understand.
Our bodies are different translations of the same ancient text,
running 18 hours a day for decades on nothing
but paint fumes and a dream,
creaking knees and dry hinges shuddering.
But somewhere between the 800th all-nighter and the electrical fire
we finally said fuck it, it's time for backup.

We know it's a tall order.
Being well is a 5-billion-dollar project with no one to settle the bill.
Most days we don't feel worthy of our caretakers' overtime,
the way they crouch down to grease our joints and axels
we disdain the downshifted schedule,
the inability to haul and kiss and sprint at full tilt.

But it's worth remembering the triumph of every month
we live to see a full moon,
every time we brush our teeth when it would be easier to forget,
every load of laundry, every opened car door, every impossible
phone call.
Even when our voices are static,
something in us announces the station.
Even when we can barely pull ourselves from bed,
we refuse to sit down.
And even when we cannot see the worth in ourselves,
a friend wraps us in warmth, a letter arrives,
a 3-year old emerges from a tunnel on the yellow line,
having found new wonder in the world.

Every Moment is Frail

Every moment is frail.
The clapboards falling in, crushing the stairwell
your communion suit, smelling of cinder and rainwater
the long journey south after the storm

The house my son was born in burnt down today
I watched the fire kiss his bedroom door
stalk into the kitchen and grab the bottle by its neck,
choke it in long licks of blistering rage
and loose stale tears on the linoleum
like a cartoon mobster collapsing

I heard the anxious footsteps at the doorway
but didn't look up
our snow globe from Barbados shaking on the mantelpiece
covering my ears so as not to hear it shatter.

      My glass of red wine on the counter, never spilling.

He was a thousand tiny fires on Thursdays,
a prediction in each exhalation of chaos
and my world became smaller from the sinking pressure,
the hot fumes closing in at sharp angles.

There was no love in that house,
those caving stairs, that threadbare carpet caught like tinder
in the blessing of this fire.
You cannot ask forgiveness of a place like that.

I whispered a prayer through the numbness,
wrestled endless gauzy layers of curtain from my vision,
fought the humid smoke that refused to part and reveal the sun.

      I barely breathe anymore because of that air.

I need more people like you
to gather my skirts and force me out the door
when I am still looking back into the flames.

Hold me up now as I stagger forward.

Pause a moment at the gate for me.
I am not here to mourn, to pray, to grieve
for old photo albums and family vacations.
I am not missing him now.
I will rub the ashes on my skin and declare war.

Future

I hold my breath for you, future
because you're coming faster than I can inhale.

I taste you, in my sweat stains and salty lips
coarse paper crusting on library books with bright orange covers
my syllabi clutched against raggy t-shirts and checkered keds,
notes flaking on my fingertips, inky and licorice-stained.

I feel you, future, surfing the crest of every exuberant keynote,
gripping tight to every handshake, every tweet,
every glance held expectant and low,
peering in the mirror at a stranger,
trying to remember where we've been seen before.

I hear you, whispering earfuls of self-doubt
poking a spindly finger into my ambitions,
easily exhausted and paranoid
the change dropping through my ribcage as it struggles to expand
wide eyes, remembering how to cry.

I am using every platform—
learning to code, learning to kiss ass
taking cold showers at 5am in unfamiliar hotel rooms,
plane rides to empty conference halls in small Midwestern cities,
refusing fear when it beats persistently at my doorframe.

Because I see you, future
emerging from the deep end, your hair slicked back and full of chlorine
your breath raw and smelling of old failures
your hands calloused as you push me in head first
so that I am forced to swim.

Little Sister

When you push the car into drive on that long roll to Los Angeles,
Don't forget me.
I am digging up trinkets from time capsules to clutter your dashboard as you wind down the 405.
I am packing Tupperware pots of ramen to fill your stomach while your spirit subsists on pure ambition.
I am writing you poems full of light for the nights when the real world is a dark place full of overdue electric bills.

When you're chasing the short end of a rainbow
to the tune of $9 an hour,
remember that you have been dreaming of California before you ever put your pinky finger on the dotted line of a jet stream,
and Pittsburgh was always an overbearing aunt repeatedly shortening your curfew.
Put your stubbornness where it will always be useful.
Hold tight to every spare paper napkin you steal from work, because you never know which one has an agent's number under the grease stain.

Treasure your graveyard shifts, your stale ham sandwiches, because freedom tastes best
when it's 40% off and a little crusty around the edges.
And make peace with your own bad habits, because they are the only things that travel with you down the whole damn runway of life.

Little sister, you have always been brimming with adventures,
so it doesn't surprise me that $400 and the open road is your idea of the American dream,
but I will always make sure there is a couch to crash into when your breaks give out and it is time for a pit stop on the long and pockmarked road trip you're taking to famous.

Don't ever doubt that I am already drafting your biography.
I have watched you conduct a whole concert dance with a broken toe,
hurl yourself bodily across 10 feet of marley with your eyes closed, smiling.

I have seen you cherry bomb on loose gravel at a 20 degree football game we weren't even winning.
And I have watched you hit so hard your elbow made a waterfall of some girl's brand new nose job.

Little sister, you are bad news for anyone who says "can't"

Never be afraid to fail at being something extraordinary
because it is always beautiful to watch you reach for the baseball that
just grazes the ridge of your fingertips,
and if you decide you prefer batting mitts to pirouettes,
I will buy you the next plane ticket to left field where your dreams have always been a long fly ball to because.

Why? I don't know. (He's on third)
but you give a damn
at least enough to refuse compromise when it offers you comfortable but you demanded remarkable.

Dreaming is heavy work, and I know
there might be months when we don't talk at all and that's ok
I remember you when you were too small to say my name,
and I remember you when you were too stubborn to need it.
I will remember your voice two years after it cuts out across the static of a transatlantic pay phone,
and I will be waiting to pick you up at the airport when the telegram comes in saying
"Home Sunday. I miss you."

But before you drive off into your movie screen sunset,
before each of us nods a discomfited hello to impending adulthood,
here are all the letters I couldn't find the postage for,
the words that never escaped my bedroom while I was penning the script of my own independence.
Let me write "I'm sorry" over all the skin I bruised with my angry pride.
Let me scratch a tally in our friendship for every time I didn't see the marks you made to let the pain seep out,
    all the times I turned my back on your crying,
    all the times I liked the taste of my own success so much I never left you a bite.

Sometimes I still don't know what I'm doing.

So let's do something neither one of us is good at so we stop competing.
Let's ride our bikes down the pier at Santa Monica and rescue sand crabs in plastic buckets.
Let's buy the ugliest pants at Goodwill and wear them to the White House.
Let's commandeer shopping carts in the Kmart parking lot and crusade across the asphalt.

Little sister, let us always be too "grownup" for this fighting.
and too young to regret the roads we never traveled,
the price of times we refused to dance with one another.
There will always be old baggage mixed with our boxes of future,
and sometimes they will be too jumbled to sort.
Gather every dream you have room for in your arms, and know that I am right behind you,
driving the Uhaul with the second load.

To John Irving, On the Day of my Grandfather's Funeral

"In the world according to Garp,
we are all terminal cases"
but the velocity at which
we approach the end
is augmented by our faith
in ordinary things:

my grandfather's necktie,
his three pack of camels and silver ashtray
the containers of his idleness and dreaming

We believe in the sanctity of these tokens,
our lives contained in their remembrance
the stories they tell about birth and journey,
recovering small miracles.

Your novel is full of these fragments:
a dressmaker's dummy brought to life
a naked gear shift, the shadow of a picture frame,
a lost baseball.

And in the end, the fragment is the story,
weaving the bittersweet ending, the moral in understated typeset,
finding meaning in old allusions, forgotten prophecy.

But where does my grandfather go?
to some place beyond his 50 years of unremarkable wandering,
fingering newspaper clippings,
polishing his toolkit and waving down the 7:45 F train
to the yards.
His thumbprints were etched with coal dust
and he was never grand.
Wouldn't go to war.
Married young and left her behind
with all his books.

My grandfather's objects tell stories for someone else,
the generations beget by his pension

blankets worn thin under his workman hands,
a wife waiting cautiously for the beginning of adventure,
both settling for the promise of their children's happiness.

In the great American novel,
this is where my grandfather belongs,
the shadow that inquires after greatness
instilling meaning with his absence—
my doctoral thesis
my sister's alcoholism
my mother, staring absently at the sky.

If we are his fragments,
then the story anticipates a poetic ending:
a wish whispered to the night air
over the rhythm of the cider house churning;
a good, smart bear for a simple hotel by the sea.

But we can only be the heroes we make room for,
and my grandfather left too much space.
I won't go searching for the inscription in his Sunday watch,
or the meaning in his untouched Phillips head;
only write the eulogy he charted for us all:
Sorrow floats, as does love.

Afghan Vacation

"Every man I fought was the hero of his own story"
he says after his third glass of wine
in the mellow hum of a San Francisco bar;
all 300 pounds of muscle in a fedora and jacket
who saw himself—twice—in the mirror of a battle
a sea of keffiyas, heads bowed in prayer and vigilance
the inscrutable other

and watched the owner of his other face crumple,
drop away into the mountains without a name or an epitaph
Another enemy disappears into the horizon
Perhaps for the better.

Bro

I grew up in a house with no windows
only mirrors
        reflections of my sister drilling dégagés in the basement,
        my mother pressing 120 with dumbbells on a slow day,
and my coaches with no time
 for sonnets composed
between swim laps.

I was 90th percentile in English but also on the scale,
my family simmering low fat margarine and skinless chicken breasts
        but forgetting to render a daughter
        who eats only to make herself happy.
My mother taught me lifting the way most girls learned mascara,
with precision and laughter,
sculpting sets in the science of interval
                            and contraction,
proposing a womanhood
so different from the blooming bodies at the community pool
all sun and hips and smooth torsos.

I decided I didn't want for that for myself,
        too busy to be beautiful anyway,
my mother brushed my hair and said I was perfect but
        when she looked in the mirror
        only saw her own last 5 pounds.

I didn't learn to move until years later,
after I'd resigned to this awkward body I was gifted,
found a lover who embraced its folds and softness,
held me erotic and I chose to believe her.

I stopped looking for that cocktail dress
        answered a heartsong for pole dancing,
            unwrapped a sexuality parceled with shoulders so sore
       I couldn't lift my arms above my head.

                And I love the ache.

Two years later and I kept dancing
        and climbing

               and spinning and aching,
lost myself in the company of beautiful women with bodies borne proudly bare,
rubbed raw and admiring our own kaleidoscopic bruises
—those war wounds of new triumph—
and suddenly I had grown a skin thick with calluses and sinew.
Who knew these muscles were roiling under all that shame?

And let me tell you it hurt like hell—and not just my body—
when my hips decided that they
       couldn't absorb any more drops and tears,
       that my muscles were packing their suitcases
       for a permanent vacation from dancing
and I would have to find some other way to exorcise the demons
from my aching joints.

Despondency found lifting like the other half of my ego,
vain and proud and competent
       unafraid of muscle expanding,
              my arms growing outward
              filling shirtsleeves to bursting
as I remembered old formulas for a space where I stand equal to men.

I know the rules to this game,
and I can push you heaving and sweating through those last 3 reps,
and I will work in on your superset
and alternate my compound movements,
my muscles leaking and crying and shaking because I am working hard.

So forgive me if you sit on the leg press with your ipod for 20 minutes,
because I will begin to doubt myself:
       maybe no mother ever taught you how to pyramid your
       weight or where to set your feet
and maybe
       you're not sure if your trick knee can take this angle,
…but also maybe
you are that pretty girl from 9th grade
 that said "I don't lift because I don't want to get bulky"
and to that, I say,

fuck you, I am a **bro**,

because I have earned every inch of the six pack you line with
chocolate sauce and kisses in the dark,
and I have fought for a body that does not say "alien" when I greet it,
and I have rejoiced in a force that builds my power
        instead of pairing
                me
                      down,
and when my friend says my legs are like tree trunks, I have to smile
and say thank you
because someone finally sees that I am a fucking redwood.

So when you say "bro" and your voice is tinged with anger or fear
I have to assume it is because you never saw
the chubby girl in second hand sweatpants
bound from the water like a silverfish,
        never watched me raise my body like Christ
            on a chrome pole in a twisted grip handspring,
never felt the bruises from goblet squats with the bar digging
grooves in my elbow pads.
Because then you would know that I wear "bro" like the same
rainbow girl scout badge as "queer"
because it makes you uncomfortable to watch a woman
who looks in the mirror
                and SEES herself,
because sometimes my fears are those same inadequacies of men:
deltoids that deflate like toy balloons
that antique dresser I expect myself to lift,
and my pride is in the same hubris of heavy things:
knowing that if the fire alarm rings, I can carry you from the
burning building to safety on my shoulders.

And there is no shame in wanting a body that maintains me.
No crime in dancing with hips that roll and spin,
no fault in cresting above the waves with the strength of my kick,
no hurt in laughing loud
        to ease the pain as I break down my muscle
        with one
                last
                      press:
I will return stronger for it tomorrow.

Unsure

Raindrops like stardust
on the panes of windows I'm not supposed to notice
have cracked open, catching ash and dust and breeze,
and forgetting,
silk shirts patted down to the curve of breast on the woman
I am supposed to respect for her mind and not her body
and mud puddles where I see my reflection for the first time.

The storm is framing my movie-kisses, my lazy Sundays,
my French toast and Earl Grey tea in bed,
when I am supposed to give her coffee and send her
on the road back to the home I didn't ask about.

The storm is soaking the edges of my blue jeans,
frayed corners suctioning rainwater up to my knees
as I watch her walk away with my umbrella.

Rain falls on the farm of my host mother
in Ukambani like a prayer
breaking the heat waves and coating the foreheads
of Mutheu and Zangi, laughing and sticking their tongues out
for the last drop.

The storm is holding back the edges of becoming,
making me wish I did not want them now when I am
so unsure.

Meeting You the Second Time

I have not seen you in three months,
but your arms have been seeking me
in the pages of a book which continues to write itself,
this absence simply making space for our bodies rehearsing:
our lips effortless as they found each other's faces
our intuition guiding hands to the pressure of new contours
as if we have always been holding each other gently on a mountaintop,
always sucking deep each other's damp night air
always waking beside the other with the sunrise,
the timepieces of our bodies clicking; synchronized

When you stroke my face and say *I see you* with palms that hush my terror
I have to believe it because you have held my entire heart on the blade of your nails
yet never cracked my skin
and without blinking, you can tell which of my poems are personal pains and which
are the stories I tell myself late at night about lovers I have never met.
There are so many ways I want to talk to you tonight,
inviting the conversations our bodies have without words
your scent like gingersnap, lingering inside me,
on the filaments of my lungs and the ridges of my mouth.

I can't *not* write you
because your eyes trace the edges of my every ordinary moment,
send my pen sprawling observations like the crisp tips of your hair brushing,
the grit of my knuckles dissolving,
your sweet milk skin rushing over me like breakfast, lunch, and dinner
because I ate you for every meal and never felt hungry.

In 4 days, you unearthed a thousand intimacies,
outlining new chapters of my gender with your cock,
riding my muscle and bone to climax, consecrating my queerness
as you pressed love into my skin, kissing every pore with your salt

and mapping me with your tongue, seeking every flavor to taste.

I wanted to craft this visit with stardust and wetness,
graft your orgasms one to the next beneath my pliant tongue
but you found layers within me and offered them back,
gave me your body over and over, roiling,
absorbed my teeth and my fists and grew bruised for that pleasure,
heavy-lidded and sighing *i like being your slut*
and I swear I nearly came from your words alone, they were so sweet.

So when you bled for me, your lip bitten anxious and unsure,
I came with a murky present,
that dark cup holding all of my stains
and said *use me [if you want]* with my eyes downcast and murmuring.
You stood on the linoleum, frowning at your own raw edges
thinking perhaps you couldn't do this after all,
yet somehow your body wanted every piece of me
absorbed my fingers like rainwater and expanded,
your fibers releasing, life blood pulsing under fingertips and through cunts
so that I pull out, gasping—humid and sweet-smelling.

And that night you gave me your wristband,
slipped on four years of history from those days when you weren't sure
what kind of future you could cobble together with heartaches and canvas,
yet you hung on with fingers strong like testimony,
your voice only wavering a little
as you stood before hundreds who couldn't see your scars unless you let them
-- And you did --
that offering blessed my workman hands,
because now I am part of *your* movement
and my elbows can prop you up when you have burned through so many iterations of your phoenix soul
and my chest can nurse justice in you when the darkness rolls on too thick.

And I would carry you to the shower with your eyes still crusted from sleep,

wash you every day until the shadows cease to crawl across your skin,
wash you every day to sooth the burning in your brain from all that oxygen running,
wash you every day knowing that depression never leaves us fully,
only hangs a Do Not Disturb sign while it sleeps to avoid the sun,
but I would wash you anyway until some of the layers of sadness sloughed off.

Which is why I know I can offer you my neck tonight,
my chin tilted defiantly skyward, like Nero facing the Romans unafraid,
for you to wrap your tender muscles around my airways and breathe me,
turn my voice to god-like spasms, whispering *fuckfuckfuck*
with every new imagining of your body,
the way I declared *love your hips, I love your belly, I love your sex, I love your thighs and your knees and your toes* without ever speaking repetition or falsehood.

So I stayed up all night memorizing you with my fingers,
tracing your cheekbones until I knew the shading,
arresting daylight with my inspections, resonant and soft,
until I was sure that I would remember you like this:
breathing deep and even into your pillows
never fearing the coming of dawn.

But when it's time to go, you have that way of shoving sandpaper against my heart
to make sure that I feel it every time you wink goodbye
because you have to gift me a little levity with this sendoff
or my chest might always be too heavy to lift itself onto the tarmac and wave,
like the Lorax rising into the sky,
hoping someone else could take on saving the world for a while,
because I am so busy loving you that I need to rest the whole ride home.

But this economy bedroom feels so empty when I rise
that some mornings I don't have the spoons to miss you
and I cry because your voice weighs more than I can carry to the kitchen

my hands shaking when I reach out for you and find only whispers,
yet those are the nights when you come to me with a handful of forks and knives
saying *I don't have the right stuff either, but without you I probably wouldn't even eat dinner.*

I guess it's the perfectionist in me
that wants to cook up a poem so rich that it overwhelms your tongue and you never want for another.
I want to explain spices to you from turmeric to cayenne and put them in a ring box
so that I can propose a world of sweet curries and stew
that bubble over and soak the walls with their scent.

And that's how I know we'll work out in the end,
because I can't tie this poem up neatly with butcher paper and string,
you keep crafting new chapters faster than I can catch the pages
so the verses pile up like all the dirty dishes we'll leave in the sink while we're fucking
and I will Never Ever stop writing you.

Thank you...

Ash Hall
Michael Sinko
Mariam Nek
Frances Reed
Jessica VonDyke
George Gordon
Eugenia Luo
Kay McMonigal
Aileen George
Avory Faucett
David Belyea
Laura Stiles
Alexis Geeza
Cassidy Kavanaugh
John Fellers
Julia Sanders
Michelle Weiner
Cassandra Perry
Alex Morgan
Ignacio Rivera
Crista Anne Orenda
Val Orenda
Joan Llanes
Michael Terry Everett
Jenn Yu Golden
Gus Golden
Lillian Nguyen
Brian O. Koyoo
Marshall Duer-Balkind
Aries Indenbaum
Lauren Mitten
Kait Scalisci

Beth Kitchin
Lance Rhinehart
Ruth Conrad
Harjant Gill
Kathy Evans-Palmisano
Jerry Palmisano
Dana Palmisano
Gail Evans-Potter
Ken Potter
Betty Evans
Amanda Lindamood
Dave Myles
Zachary Skigen
Alex Demas
Ashley Burnside
Ginger Yachinich
Joyce Washington
Courtney Morgan
Carla Marina Carreira
Victor Mwanza
Lydia Sabina
JoEllen Notte
Sarah Miller
Julian Dockhorn
Stevia Morawski
Julia Sanders
Jackie Reese
Jesus Chavez
Laura Steiner
Shadeen Francis
Ashley Truxal
Danielle Foote

...and so many other inspiring people that have touched my life.

Bianca Palmisano is a queer poet, dancer, and sex educator based out of Washington, DC. She is the author of another poetry volume, "The Empty Spaces" and several short stories. She runs the healthcare education company, Intimate Health Consulting, which trains medical providers on how to address sexual health and minority health in clinical practice. "Will This Be On the Final?" is her second poetry volume.

www.ingramcontent.com/pod-product-compliance
Lightning Source LLC
Chambersburg PA
CBHW031416040426
42444CB00005B/602